Original title:
Gravity's a Drag

Copyright © 2025 Creative Arts Management OÜ
All rights reserved.

Author: Elias Montgomery
ISBN HARDBACK: 978-1-80567-822-9
ISBN PAPERBACK: 978-1-80567-943-1

When Gravity Kisses the Sky

When I jump, I float like a feather,
But down I crash, 'cause we're tethered.
I try to dance on the ceiling rare,
Yet land on my butt with a comical flair.

I've got a friend who thinks he can fly,
He leaps off the couch, oh my oh my!
He aims for the stars but hits the floor,
Next time he'll think twice, I'm sure!

A squirrel in the tree, plotting his route,
Spots a stray dog and lets out a shout.
He jumps in the air with a goofy grin,
But thuds on the branch, where's the win?

Let's toss our cares, like shoes in the air,
But down they come, oh what a scare!
In this world where we float and fall,
We laugh at our stumbles, oh isn't that all?

Heavy Hearts and Light Minds

In a world where worries spin,
Laughter bubbles from within.
We juggle all our heavy thoughts,
But joy's the prize that can't be bought.

Chasing dreams just like a kite,
With giggles shining, hearts so light.
We bounce on clouds, we trip and fall,
'Tis silliness that conquers all.

Descent into Serenity

Floating down like autumn leaves,
I laugh at what my heart believes.
A tumble here, a slip over there,
But who can frown with wind to share?

As I tumble, I'm not alone,
With pals who make this journey known.
Life's a ride, so hold on tight,
And enjoy the flight into the night.

Clouds Too Heavy to Carry

Up above, those clouds look grim,
Yet I wear a highly polished grin.
They peek down with their heavy sighs,
But I just wink, and then I fly.

What could be worse than losing cheer?
So play with troubles, hold them near.
Tickle them 'til they dissolve,
In laughter, all our woes evolve.

Moonlit Melancholy

The moon's a smile, bright on the ground,
While I stumble in thoughts profound.
With shadows dancing, I take a chance,
In the twilight, I join the prance.

Each pondered frown turns to a jest,
For who can ponder with such zest?
In the night, I float and sway,
Finding joy in the blues of play.

Weightless Whispers

In the sky, I do a flip,
Floating high, on a whim I trip.
Clouds giggle while I glide,
In this dance, I cannot hide.

Jumping jacks in mid-air bliss,
My feet just can't find their kiss.
Laughter echoes, a silly sound,
As I bounce all around.

Silly hats and balloons bright,
Making friends with stars at night.
A cosmic game, it's pure delight,
A wobbly waltz, oh what a sight.

Catch me now, I'm on the hunt,
For the moon's sweet, milky font.
But down I fall with a great big thud,
Into a bowl of cosmic mud.

When the Earth Tugs Too Strong

Oh dear Earth, with your tight embrace,
Can't you let me find my space?
Every leap is just a tease,
I'm stuck here, down on my knees.

Bounce, bounce, like a rubber ball,
Each attempt ends in a fall.
The sidewalk cracks up with glee,
As I land – oh not again, oh me!

Chasing dreams like they're a kite,
But that tug pulls with all its might.
My feet cling to the pavement tight,
While my hopes take graceful flight.

Why can't I run, or skip away?
Every pull wants me to stay.
With every giggle, a new day found,
I'll dance with my shoes glued to the ground.

Dancing with the Fallen

Leaves whirl like a slow ballet,
Each one winking – come, let's play!
I twirl and spin, a joyful spree,
But the ground just laughs at me.

A tumble here, a stumble there,
I'm a circus act without a care.
The trees all cheer, 'Go on, take flight!'
But my feet keep saying, 'Not tonight!'

With a cap on my head, I take a chance,
Then trip over roots in a wild dance.
Laughter bubbles from roots below,
As I become part of the show.

The ground's a friend; we giggle and sigh,
With every flop, I reach for the sky.
If falling's the path, I'll wear it proud,
In the company of the laughing crowd.

The Pull of Unraveled Dreams

Each wish I make, it floats away,
Caught in the breeze like a game to play.
I leap to grab but start to slide,
My dreams now have nowhere to hide.

Unraveled yarns, like kites in flight,
Tangled up in the moonlight.
I chase the stars with all my might,
But once again, I miss tonight.

A trampoline of hopes and fears,
Bouncing high, till laughter clears.
I drift above, but oh, such fun,
Till gravity's grip says I'm done.

So here I lie, on the soft green grass,
Wishing for wings to fly, alas!
Though I'm tethered here, I'll still have glee,
For in this folly, I'm truly free.

Pull Me Under

I tried to jump, it felt so right,
But down I went, oh what a sight!
The sidewalk laughed, the sky just spun,
As I became a soil-bound one.

My shoes are heavy, my hopes are light,
I thought I'd soar, but took a bite.
Now all I do is watch the stars,
While tethered here with earth-bound cars.

Heavy Dreams

I had a dream I flew so high,
But woke to find my butt's awry.
The pillow hugged, it wouldn't let,
No wings in sight, just daily fret.

My bed a trap, sheets like lead,
I'm sleeping sound, but dream instead.
No magic carpets in my room,
Just morning coffee and broom.

Light Steps

I tiptoe round with caution keen,
With every step, my socks turn green.
I tried to bounce, but fell instead,
A trampoline? No, it's my bed.

I dance with dust, I sway with sound,
But gravity's the star around.
At parties, I'll just hug the floor,
While everyone else wishes for more.

Breaking Free from the Chains

I wiggled free, but oh, not quite,
My belt's too tight, what a delight!
I think I'll stretch; oops, there it goes,
The waistband snaps, oh how it shows!

I've tried to run, but tripped on air,
Those heavy legs, they don't play fair.
I'm breaking free, now isn't it fun?
But now I'm tangled, oh what a run!

The Night's Intense Embrace

The moonlit path can seem so bright,
Until you trip and lose your sight.
With twinkling stars that start to wink,
My feet just seem to miss the link.

The dark can hug with weight so tight,
I stumble through, but feel delight.
I laugh aloud at my own fate,
As night's embrace just seals my state.

Pull of Yesterday

Float like a feather, I jumped into air,
But landed right back, felt the weight of despair.
My shoes are like anchors, they won't let me soar,
I guess the past really knows how to snore.

A trampoline's magic, it tries for a fling,
Yet here I am grounded, still waiting for spring.
Chasing my dreams with a trampoline bounce,
But my feet find the floor; the joke's on my flounce.

The Balance Between Worlds

A dance at the edge of a soft springy floor,
Where laughter collides with a loud 'no more!'
One step to the left, I'm flying in glee,
Then boom! I'm grounded, oh why won't you free me?

My socks are conspirators, slippery and sly,
They giggle and wiggle, 'Oh give it a try!'
I teeter on chaos, a curious blend,
Of giggles and tumbles, my own comic end.

When the Ground Calls

The ground has a voice, it whispers my name,
It beckons and pulls me, it's such a bad game.
I bounce with a giggle, then 'splat!', on my face,
Saying, 'Maybe the sky wasn't my place!'

I dream of a dance with the clouds up above,
But they shake their heads, saying, 'Take that, my love!'
So promptly I tumble, a laugh and a fall,
Embracing the chaos, I cradle it all.

Flashes of Weightlessness

When I jump with a leap, I feel like a kite,
But gravity's tether pulls back with a bite.
In moments of lightness, I giggle and sway,
Yet back to the ground, it just has to play.

Like feathers and pies in a windstorm's embrace,
I float in the chaos, a strange weightless race.
Moments so silly, I'm spinning in air,
With laughter I tumble—a jester's affair.

The Downward Spiral

Falling down the stairs again,
I swear I've got a plan.
Gravity pulls, it makes me trip,
My balance is a rickety ship.

Balloons float high with glee,
While I'm stuck at knee degree.
Every step feels like a rhyme,
As I stumble through space and time.

A plummet's just a slip of fate,
Time's a trickster, oh so great.
When I fall, it's quite the show,
Like a clown with nowhere to go.

But when I land, I laugh and say,
"Guess I'm grounded, come what may!"
An acrobat without the flair,
Just a jester in mid-air.

Threads of Resistance

I tried to jump a little high,
But my shoes just said goodbye.
Off the couch, I felt a pull,
Like a rollercoaster, oh so dull.

Every leap is met with scorn,
As I knock down things I'd worn.
The cat gives me a sideways glance,
It seems I'm high on broken chance.

I wear my cape, but still I fall,
Like a superhero with a ball.
Each attempt a funny jest,
I'm a hero, but not the best.

Yet in the mess, a joy I find,
In the chaos, I unwind.
For every trip, there's laughter loud,
In my antics, I am proud.

Earthbound Echoes

Bouncing on the trampoline,
I swear I'm feeling lean and mean.
But the ground has other plans,
Pulling me back with heavy hands.

With every jump, my spirit flies,
Yet down I come, oh how I sigh.
Like a rubber band, I stretch and snap,
Landed flat—what a mishap!

The birds above, they tease and chirp,
While I wiggle, trying to burp.
They soar high with effortless ease,
While I'm elbow-deep in dirt and leaves.

Still, laughter floats with each leap caught,
I'm the joker in this gravity plot.
Earth's embrace may feel like a trap,
But I'll bounce up, ready to clap!

Tides of Tenacity

Surfing through the crowded room,
As I dodge and weave, I zoom.
But gravity plays a nasty trick,
And I trip on a coiled cord—oh slick!

I rise again with a chuckle loud,
Despite the trials, I'm oh so proud.
With every tumble, I gain a grin,
The dance of life is where I win.

Why walk when I can skip and slide?
It's all a game I won't abide.
Dancing while the ceiling spins,
Each wobble, laugh, my joy begins.

So let the world pull me down tight,
I'll find a way to laugh and fight.
As I sway through life's mad spree,
It's a riot, you'll agree!

Below the Surface of Stillness

When I dive in the pool, I float like a leaf,
But my belly's a whale; oh, what a relief!
The stillness is sweet, till I make a splash,
Now the lifeguard's looking, I better act brash.

Bubbles rise up, in a dance with my toes,
While my goggles fog up, oh, how it shows!
Fins on my feet, I'm a fishy delight,
Until I trip backwards, it's a comical sight.

My friends cheer me on, "You could swim like a cat!"
I chuckle and giggle, just look at this spat!
A dive of delight, but the surface won't stay,
As I bob back to comfort and laugh all the way.

With each clumsy stroke, I ignore the sheer force,
Laughing at life, the best kind of course!
Above the calm waters, my troubles all cease,
While I splosh and I flop, I find my own peace.

The Weight We Bear

Bouncing on scales, it's a comical sight,
Counting those snacks, oh what a delight!
Each piece of chocolate, a weight to behold,
Yet my heart feels lighter, as stories unfold.

Running in circles, like a dog on a chase,
The pounds they are stubborn, but I keep up the pace!
With every big step, I'm a dancer on land,
Spinning and twirling—this weight just can't stand!

Friends say I'm crazy, a whirlwind of fun,
But laughter's the lightest, so here I still run.
Let the cookies pile up, my joy goes before,
Weightless in spirit, forever I soar!

Weights, they can't hold me, I'm soaring like air,
In a world full of giggles, there's plenty to share.
So raise a loud cheer, let the calories culminate,
Life's far too short to worry and wait!

Chasing the Weightless

I chased after clouds; they danced in the blue,
Thought I could reach them, if I only knew.
Jumping and reaching, I'm a kid on the run,
With dreams of the sky, oh, this is pure fun!

The breeze whispers tales, of flying so high,
With my arms stretched out, just to tickle the sky.
I leap and I twirl, it's a comical race,
But gravity's tricky, keeps me in my place!

My friends shake their heads, "You've got to be light!"
As I wiggle and jiggle under soft Luna's light.
"Just float like a feather, and float on the breeze,"
So I set off to giggle, with elegance and ease.

Then I tumble and flounder, a laugh in my fall,
Still chasing those clouds, oh, I'm having a ball!
While some fly away, I just want to play,
Life's all about joy, let's dance 'til we sway!

Gravity of the Heart

My heart's like a balloon, it bounces with glee,
But when I see dessert, it drops right to me!
With every sweet bite, my spirits take flight,
As I skip and I hop, from morning till night.

Friends gather 'round, as we share in the cheer,
"Who needs a gym when there's laughter right here?"
With our bellies a-jiggle and smiles from ear to ear,
We find joy in the baking, there's nothing to fear!

A tug on my heart like a magnet, it pulls,
To frosted delights, all those cake-filled bowls.
Yet the laughter remains, like a light in the dark,
When we share in our stories, and eat 'til we spark!

So let's lift up our forks, and forget all our woes,
With the weight of our joy, let's see how it grows.
Our hearts are all light, with a chuckle or two,
For everything's better when shared with a crew!

Floating Through the Chaos

In the air, I try to soar,
My shoes weigh more than before.
I tumble, roll, then hit the ground,
Is this the fun of spinning 'round?

With each leap, I plot my flight,
But gravity gives me quite a fright.
I flail my arms, I twist and spin,
With every bounce, where to begin?

My dog thinks it's a game to play,
Chasing me in a comical way.
I call for help, but no one's near,
Just me and laughter, full of cheer.

I'm floating high, just for a bit,
Until the earth says, "Time to sit!"
But I'll keep dreaming of the skies,
While waving to the solid pies.

The Art of Letting Go

I took a dive into the blue,
Thought I'd float, but who knew?
With one quick bounce, I hit the floor,
Next time I'll plan this better, for sure!

The trampoline is calling me,
I swear I'm light as a bumblebee.
But mid-air giggles lead to a flop,
Well, at least I know I'll never stop!

I try to fly with grace and zest,
Instead, I become a laughing jest.
With every plunge, my confidence swells,
In this comedy, who really tells?

So here I am, fleeting and free,
In this circus of absurdity.
I let go, smile, and let it flow,
Embracing the chaos, putting on a show.

Shadows in Suspension

My shadow lifts, it wants to play,
But it won't float too far away.
We dance on sidewalks, skip and prance,
Yet every jump gives it a chance!

High above, the birds do tease,
While I'm stuck with knees like cheese.
I wave to clouds that gently drift,
While I'm earthbound, give them a lift!

A trampoline calls out my name,
I leap and holler, it's all a game.
I fly like comedy on a spree,
Landing back with gravity to agree.

But there's humor in this pull and grasp,
As I chase my dreams in a joyful clasp.
With laughter echoing in my ears,
I keep on bouncing through the years!

When the Sky Feels Heavy

The clouds are thick, like pillows round,
 Dripping dreams down to the ground.
  I feel the weight of silly thoughts,
 Trying to float like summer yachts.

 Balloons escape my clumsy hands,
  As I fumble through cotton land.
 A cloud says, "Come, take a ride!"
 But I trip over my own wild stride.

 With each attempt to lift and glide,
  I taste the laughter I can't abide.
Why does the Earth want me to stay?
  Can't it see I'm fun to sway?

I dance in rain that plops and splats,
While umbrellas fall like kitty cats.
So here we go, let's laugh and sing,
 In this bizarre and funny fling!

Floating in Earth's Embrace

In the sky, I try to float,
Like a balloon, just with my coat.
But down I go, much to my dread,
Earth's got a grip on my big head.

I leap and think I'll soar so high,
But down I come with a goofy sigh.
The universe laughs, what a grand show,
While I dance like a marionette below.

I dream of clouds, they seem so sweet,
But find myself back on my feet.
Feet so heavy, no wings to spread,
I guess I'll stick to my comfy bed!

In dreams I fly, with style and flair,
But waking life is just unfair!
With every bounce, I hit the ground,
Oh, how I long to spin around.

Chain of Celestial Constraints

Stars above with twinkling lights,
They tease me with their lofty heights.
I try to jump, to reach the moon,
But end up pulling a silly tune.

With each attempt to break free,
The cosmos chuckles, oh so glee.
I'm tethered here, no chance to roam,
Just a merry fool, far from home.

I imagine I could sail the space,
Yet here I am, a grounded face.
The ground it holds me, like a pet,
With dreams that soar, but I'm not set!

So I spin and twirl, a funky game,
While everything laughs at my name.
A cosmic joke, oh what a bind,
Chained to the earth, where fun's aligned.

Defying the Silent Pull

I launch my body, arms spread wide,
But end up plummeting from the ride.
The pull of earth, it just won't stop,
As I comet-ly crash, like a soda pop!

I donned a cape, thought I could fly,
But birds just chuckled as I passed by.
With every leap, a thud, a flop,
The ground's my friend, or maybe a cop!

I dance around like it's all a game,
Yet every fall is pretty lame.
I try to glide, on air I chant,
But alas, I'm just a clumsy plant!

So here I stand, a jester's plight,
Chasing dreams in a comic flight.
The silent pull, a wicked jest,
But I'll keep laughing, that's my quest!

Too Close to the Currents

With every gust, I flail and sway,
Like a leaf caught in a wild ballet.
I think I'll fly, but whoops, not me!
Just a twirl in the wind, oh can't you see?

A tumble here, a spin there too,
A circus act for the pigeons to view.
I ride the waves of an unseen stream,
But mostly wake up from my wacky dream!

The sun looks down, it giggles away,
"This isn't how you fly," it seems to say.
With every gust, I'm slammed around,
Catching air like a silly hound!

I chase horizons and wave to the trees,
But still find myself down on my knees.
Too close to the currents, giving me fright,
As I tumble and spin, in pure delight!

Tumbling Through the Atmosphere

I tried to leap, but tripped on air,
My feet left ground, but oh! I swear.
A bird did laugh, I waved goodbye,
As I was launched, like a pie gone fly.

The clouds are soft, like marshmallow fluff,
Bouncing around, though it gets quite tough.
I laugh aloud, what a silly sight,
Down I go, hoping I'll be all right.

Up high I see a sandwich float,
I'm on a ride, a flying boat.
The wind's my friend, though it's a tease,
It plays with hair, just like a breeze.

So here I am, just drifting high,
Like a cloud, I wish I could fly.
But down I fall, like a drooping leaf,
And oh my friend, it's quite a belief!

Tethered Desires

I wanted to soar, to dance and tease,
But back to the ground, I'm stuck like cheese.
With dreams that float and fears that cling,
I'm like a puppet on a string.

The balloons I tied, they rose with glee,
But I'm weighed down, oh woe is me!
I chased a kite, it took to flight,
I followed hard, with all my might.

The tug of fun pulls me back down,
Like a jester stuck in a frown.
Oh, to be free, just one sweet leap,
But tethered here, my dreams won't keep.

So here I stand, on solid ground,
With wishes floating all around.
I'll take a bow, for this bumbling show,
Then dream of the day I'll float like snow!

When the Stars Feel Tangible

I reach for stars, they wink and tease,
Close enough to grab, but not with ease.
A comet flips, and does a spin,
I trip on thoughts, where to begin?

With stardust dreams, I paint the sky,
But like a chicken, I just can't fly.
I'm up on tips, I stretch and sway,
Yet fall to earth like yesterday.

The Milky Way is just a stream,
I splash about, it's like a dream.
Oh sweet moon, with your cheesy glow,
I'm dancing under, just so slow.

Stars giggle bright, they twinkle down,
While I get tangled, lost in the town.
I'll keep on leaping, high and far,
Until I catch a shooting star!

The Drift of Distant Dreams

I sailed a thought on a breeze so light,
Chasing it down, oh what a sight!
But dreams can drift, like soap bubbles,
Floating away, wrapped in troubles.

I built a castle from silly schemes,
But it crumbled fast, those pesky beams.
I laughed so hard, with dreams in tow,
Yet still they floated, much too slow.

Clouds unruly, they tickle my nose,
I chase them still, where no one knows.
Whispers of wishes, playful and sweet,
Fly off my head, like candy, neat.

So I keep leaping, a little absurd,
Spinning and twirling, a dizzy bird.
With dreams that drift, I'll tread the breeze,
And revel in giggles, oh how they please!

The Silent Weight of Existence

In the morning, I rise, like a loaf,
  my bread dough dreams can't stay afloat.
  Each step feels heavy, like I'm in a race,
  but I trip and tumble, it's a clumsy chase.

  My thoughts are balloons, stuck to the ground,
  they float away slowly, not making a sound.
  I try to be light, like a feather in flight,
  but my socks keep creeping, what a silly plight!

  The coffee is bold, much like my fate,
  it brings me back down to a caffeinated state.

  In a world of chaos, I can almost see,
  that the weight of existence is just tea with me.

  So I laugh at the floor, it's part of the fun,
  the pull of the earth, I can't really run.
  I'll dance with my shadows, embrace every strain,
  while dreaming of skies where I float like a plane.

Eclipsed by Reality

When I reach for my dreams, they dodge and they weave,

> like a game of charades, I can't quite believe.
> They twirl through my fingers, like soap in the air,
> while my couch keeps calling, I don't really care.
>
> The alarm clock sings songs of obligations and woes,
> but my blanket's a fortress, and nobody knows.
> I could conquer the world if I rolled out of bed,
> but instead, I've decided, to rest my poor head.

With a snack and a show, I plan my retreat,
the horizons of freedom are just out of reach.
When reality knocks, I just muffle the sound,

and giggle at life, as I lounge on the ground.

Who needs to defy when I can just lie,
an eternal homebody under the sky?
In the game of 'be light,' I play the sly ace,
eclipsed by my comfort, with cushions I brace.

Surrendering to the Pull

I'm a gumdrop stuck to the bottom of shoes,
    each wobble and jiggle brings me some blues.

    As I roll down the sidewalk, feet all around,
        I surrender to laughter, it's a sweet little sound.

    I thought I'd be graceful, like a leaf in the breeze,
but I'm more like a pancake, I flop with such ease.
The weight of the world has me bound up in fun,
    while I search for the sun, I just melt in the sun.

I'll embrace my descent with a giggle and grin,
maybe this dragging is where life will begin.
Each wobble and jiggle tells me one truth,
    that since life is a dance, I'll sway in my youth.

So here's to the pull, let it take me away,
in a tangle of laughs, I'll just sway and I'll play.
Like a ball of yarn, I'll lose all my fears,
surrendering to whimsy, I'll roll through the years.

The Drift of Days

Each day's a balloon that I try to inflate,
    but they drift with the wind, and I'm stuck with the weight.
    I muster my courage to float on the breeze,
but the ground insists on holding my knees.

    I wander through moments, from kitchen to chair,
with socks from last week, I just don't care.
    They stick to the tiles, like I'm stuck in a dream,
    where the world's just a joke, or so it may seem.

    Time slips like gelato, melting away,
    with puddles of laughter, I'll drift and I'll sway.
The hours will giggle, the minutes will tease,
    while I float in my world, oh, such sweet unease.

So here's to the days that just roll like a wave,

where the drag of my reality I willingly brave.

With a wink and a chuckle, I'll dance with the sun,
    letting each little drift be a part of my fun.

Pulling Against the Current

I'm stuck in quicksand, oh what a plight,
Trying to leave but I'm losing the fight.
With every step forward, I slide back anew,
Like a fish on dry land, what's a swimmer to do?

A tugboat of giggles drags me along,
While my friends and their laughter belt out a song.
Each time that I stumble, they cheer and they grin,
Pulling me up just to watch me fall in.

I've got a knack for flopping quite well,
A walrus on ice, just under a spell.
Yet here in the mess, I find sweetest delight,
With comrades who're crazy, we'll dance through the night.

So here's to the struggles, the slips and the slides,
With a wink and a joke, I embrace all the rides.
Life may be heavy, but laughter's the key,
Adrift in this chaos, I'm wild and I'm free.

Earthbound with Wings

With feet on the ground, I dream up a flight,
I flap my big arms in the soft morning light.
My friends all just chuckle, but I'm feeling bold,
Imagine the stories of daring retold.

A spring in my bounce, like a pogo on air,
I leap with a giggle, hoping for flair.
Yet gravity whispers, 'Oh stay where you are,'
But I'll soar through the skies, dreaming of stars.

I cling to my sandwich as birds fly above,
While searching for peanut butter, my only true love.
I wave at the clouds, they just puffily tease,
As I fumble and stumble, I'm brought to my knees.

Yet trapped on this planet, I shrug with a grin,
'Cause laughter's the ticket, and that's how I win.
I'll find all the magic from here to the moon,
With wings made of whimsy, I float to my tune.

The Teetering Dance of Life

On the tightrope of fate, I waddle and sway,
With a jester's big hat, I'm here for the play.
One foot out of line sends me tumbling down,
Yet I spring back up with a smile, not a frown.

A partner of clumsiness, twirls 'round my feet,
Yanking me sideways, can't handle the beat.
As we cha-cha and tango, I topple with grace,
The audience roars, a full-frontal embrace.

Each spin is a slip, but laughter's the key,
I pirouette wildly, my heart in a spree.
With tippy-toe antics, we waddle in glee,
For life's just a dance, full of playfulness, see?

So let's toast the stumbles, the turns and the falls,
With a grin and a giggle, we'll dance through the walls.
For in this grand circus, we're all quite absurd,
Let's flaunt our missteps, let chaos be heard!

Shadows of Heavy Hearts

In the gloom of the night, our shadows take flight,
Laughing at burdens that claim our delight.
With funny reflections, we skip on the street,
It's a circus of worries with clown feet and beat.

We trip on our dreams like they're shoes made of lead,
Yet here comes a chuckle to lighten our dread.
The more that we ponder, the funnier it gets,
As we dance with our troubles, with no time for regrets.

The weight may be heavy, but joy's on the rise,
With our feet in a shuffle, we reach for the skies.
In shadows that linger, we muster a grin,
A cabaret of chaos where laughter begins.

So let's raise our voices, let tears turn to glee,
With a wink to the moon, we'll sing wild and free.
For while life may be loaded with burdens and strife,
We'll find all the humor that dances through life.

Driftwood Dreams and Heavy Seas

On tides of laughter, we all float,
Like driftwood dancing, we take note.
With jellyfish jokes that make us grin,
We bob and weave, let the fun begin.

The sea's a stage, the waves our song,
As seagulls chuckle, we swim along.
Caught in the currents of wacky delight,
In heavy seas, our spirits take flight.

Echoes of What Remains

Lost socks tumble from shore to sea,
Echoes of laughter—just you and me.
With beach balls bouncing like wayward dreams,
The ocean whispers in silly schemes.

Shells hold secrets, but we drop hints,
Grinning at crabs as the ocean flints.
With every splash, a giggle resounds,
We stir up mischief where joy abounds.

The Tug of Hard Realities

Swimmers swim, but sinkers sink,
A tug-of-war, don't you think?
In pools of laughter, we soon can drown,
While mermaids giggle, donning their crowns.

Life's heavy stones crash down like waves,
But we're buoyant in our playful caves.
We float on jokes and dance with glee,
What's heavy now might just make us free.

A Fall Into Untold Stories

Falling for tales that twist and turn,
We take the plunge, and watch our yearn.
With splashes of ink and bubbles of fun,
Our story's just begun, we're not yet done.

As we tumble through laughter, unplanned and wild,
The land of the quirky beckons the child.
Join us in this dive, don't hesitate,
In untold stories, let's celebrate!

Carrying the Cosmos

I tried to lift the Milky Way,
But it slipped right through my hands.
The stars just giggled at my plight,
Said, "Buddy, lighten your plans!"

I strapped on Jupiter, my friend,
He bounced right off my head.
A cosmic joke played in the night,
I laughed till I turned red.

Pluto joined the party too,
But he felt a bit too small.
"I'm not a planet, you know,"
I tossed him like a ball!

And as I danced with Saturn's rings,
I tripped and took a dive.
Turns out the universe is great,
But it's hard to stay alive!

A Melancholy Tangent

I fell in love with the moonlit sky,
But it weighed a ton, I swear.
Every beam a sulking sigh,
The starry face just wouldn't care.

In a space where wishes float,
I tried to chase my dreams.
Got tangled in a comet's tail,
Life's not always what it seems.

I wrote a note to cosmic fate,
"Please lighten up my load!"
But all I got back was a wink,
And the universe just glowed.

With every step a heavy heart,
I danced in sweet despair.
The cosmos laughed at my odd art,
As I fell without a care.

Sinking into Starlight

I took a plunge into the stars,
Who knew they'd be so deep?
I thought I'd float right through the void,
But instead, I found a heap!

A black hole called my name aloud,
"Oh, come and take a ride!"
I thought I'd soar and twist around,
But ended up inside.

The sun said, "You're too heavy, friend!"
As laughter filled the space.
I tried to dance but hit the ground,
And came back with a face!

Fell flat as planets spun above,
Like pizza dough with flair.
I sipped a star on my way down,
And forgot my every care!

The Weight of Unsaid Words

With all my feelings bottled tight,
    I'd launch into the night.
But every thought turned heavy now,
    And dragged me out of sight.

I whispered secrets to the breeze,
    Hoping they'd float away.
But like a rock, they clung to me,
    And wouldn't let me play.

A comet caught my silent pleas,
    And promptly made a face.
"Let go!" it cried; "It's just a thought,
    So why the heavy chase?"

And as I pondered what to say,
    The stars began to roll.
I laughed, I cried, I pulled a face,
    Then tumbled to my soul!

Ripples in the Fabric of Air

A pancake flipped right off the floor,
It floats like dreams we can't ignore.
My shoes have wings, they start to sway,
In this topsy-turvy game we play.

The cat's defying all the laws,
She leaps and lands just because.
With fishy thoughts that swirl and glide,
Who needs a ground to run and hide?

The coffee spills, but what a sight!
It takes a tour, defying night.
I laugh at how the muffins roll,
When all they want is just a bowl.

But all is well, the sun will pop,
We'll dance on ceilings, never stop.
We'll twirl through life, no end in sight,
With heavy hearts, we're light as light.

A Leap toward Distant Stars

I strung a kite with dreams and jest,
It soared above, a clever quest.
With every leap, my socks take flight,
Into the realm of pure delight.

The moon's a target meant to catch,
But it just grins, can't make a match.
I swing my arms like I'm the breeze,
And who knew joy could come with ease?

Yet every tumble, every spin,
Just proves again what lies within.
With stars above, I wish on toes,
As gravity's humor truly shows.

So trampoline my heart's desire,
To reach the sky, fuel dreams with fire.
Like silly clouds, we float along,
In laughter's dance, where we belong.

Surrendering to the Weight of Wishes

A paper boat, it takes the plunge,
In waters deep, I feel the lunge.
Each wish a stone, they start to pile,
As hopes surrender, what a trial!

I tossed a wish, it caught some air,
And danced about without a care.
A potted plant just rolled away,
With wishes gone, it's here to stay.

I feel the tug of every thought,
As butterflies escape my rots.
They pull me down, my heart's in play,
Who needs the ground when dreams can sway?

So here I'll float, a whimsy tale,
In buoyant joy, I'll never pale.
A weightless dance on life's big stage,
Where wishes roam like a cheeky mage.

The Terrain of Longing

I tried to ski on fluffy clouds,
But I slid down, not too proud.
With every curve, I start to spin,
In pancake lands, I find my kin.

A yearning heart, a searching gaze,
In cartwheels through the endless haze.
The sunlit fields call me to play,
As I trip lightly, who needs a stay?

With every tip, every silly flip,
The world's a stage, we're on this trip.
In longing's quest, the laughter roars,
We stumble through the open doors.

So pack your dreams, don't mind the fall,
Our hearts will soar, we'll have a ball.
With every step, we giggle bright,
On this terrain, our hearts take flight.

A Dance with the Abyss

I tried to jump, I swore I'd fly,
But landed flat, oh me, oh my!
With every bounce, my hopes go high,
   Yet here I am, just asking, why?

I wore a cape, my heart a flame,
Thought I was cool, but what a shame!
The ground just laughed and called my name,
   As I tumbled down, what a silly game!

I practiced spins, I thought I'd shine,
But now I'm stuck, a worm in brine!
The stars above, they seem to whine,
   As I declare, this dance is mine!

So here's to leaps, to silly flights,
To making jokes and silly sights!
I'll leap again, with all my might,
   Until the ground rises for a bite!

Beneath the Weight of Earth

Underneath where shadows creep,
I ponder how I lost my leap.
The ground's a friend, but not too deep,
It holds me close, in dreams I sheep!

Each time I run, I feel the pull,
Like I'm a bee, and that's the hull.
I stutter-step, it's quite the lull,
Yet laughter bubbles, oh so full!

I bow to rocks, they mock my fumble,
In this unseen game, I stumble.
With every trip, the laughter's rumble,
A comedy show, where I'm the jumble!

So let me trip, let me sway,
And laugh with me, come what may!
For under weight, I find my play,
In every slip, I own the day!

Celestial Anchor

A fancy ship upon the sea,
But I forgot the laws, you see!
My anchor's stuck, I can't break free,
Exploring skies, just not for me!

Each time I launch, I hit the floor,
The cosmos laughs, and I want more.
Among the stars, I start to snore,
When back to Earth, I'm duty's chore.

I dreamed of lands where fairies dance,
But here I am, with no romance.
In every flop, there's no second chance,
My moonlit dreams, just silly prance!

So here's a toast, to all who fly,
To those who leap and kiss the sky!
Just watch your step, or you might cry,
With gravity's grip, you'll say goodbye!

The Lure of the Inky Void

I stare into that endless night,
The stars all wink, oh what a sight!
But closer in, the ground's delight,
It pulls me down, with all its might.

A cosmic dance, my heart does sing,
Yet each attempt makes my head ring.
I chase a comet, what joy it brings,
But back to earth, my tether swings!

With every bounce, I swirl and twirl,
Falling flat, giving fate a whirl.
The void calls out, a tempting pearl,
But gravity just makes me hurl!

So here I float, a dream I'd weave,
With every trip, I do believe,
The laugh of space will not deceive,
And in the sink, I dare to leave!

The Weight of Wishes

I'd fly so high, a kite in the sky,
But my dreams just seem to sigh.
With every leap, I sink like a stone,
Why can't I claim my throne?

When I skip, I feel the pull,
Like a dance that's far from dull.
My hopes are light, yet here I stand,
Just me and my dreams, unplanned.

A bounce, a jump, a rollicking chase,
Why must the ground hold me in place?
I laugh as I tumble, a clumsy bird,
My wishes are flapping, they need a word.

So here I stay, with hearts that soar,
Wishing on wishes, who could ask for more?
Up with a giggle, down with a squeal,
Oh, the weight of wishes is part of the deal!

Untethering the Soul

I tried to float like a balloon,
But my soul's still tied to a spoon.
Launched it high with a goofy grin,
It got stuck in a tree again.

I swear I saw a starry light,
But the ground called me back, 'Not tonight!'
With every step, I trip and fall,
It seems my feet just hate the sprawl.

My heart dances, it's ready to fly,
Yet my shoes are heavy, oh me, oh my!
Trying to run while stuck in place,
What a funny, silly race!

So I'll giggle and twirl, laugh at the snags,
While dreaming of fields instead of drags.
Let's untie the soul, give it a run,
With joy in the world, oh, that will be fun!

The Earth's Gravitational Hold

My feet are glued right to the floor,
I hope one day to touch the shore.
Jumping jacks with a bounce and a hop,
But here I stay, oh what a flop!

Every time I think I'm free,
Back to ground, I fall with glee.
Like a fish out of water, flailing around,
Life's too heavy, falling down.

I tried to skateboard, gave it a whirl,
But the earth just said, 'Oh, what a girl!'
Round and round, clumsy and wild,
A giggle, a stumble, a mischief child.

Yet I laugh as I cling to the ground,
Finding joy in the silly, profound.
In this chaotic, comical game,
It's the giggles and tumbles that keep me the same!

Anchored Voices

I hear my dreams whispering loud,
Yet the ground keeps me, a silly crowd.
I shout for freedom, but it's a drag,
I'm just a voice from a bouncing bag.

Each word I say just slumps down low,
Like a joke that won't start to flow.
With every try to lift, they stall,
Why can't words just bounce and sprawl?

Chasing laughter up to the sky,
But their weight's got me asking why.
I try to rise, but I keep on sinking,
A heavyweight poet, my spirits are blinking.

So I'll sing with a grin as I trip on my tongue,
While dancing with dreams that feel so young.
Voices anchored, yet I find my choice,
In the joy of the journey, I still hear my voice!

When Silence Weighs Heavy

When silence is loud, my thoughts start to dance,
They twirl and they leap in a comical prance.
I tiptoe on whispers, I giggle with glee,
As my mind throws a party, just not inviting me.

Each sigh is a balloon, floating up in the sky,
If only they'd pop, oh how I would fly!
But silence is sticky, like honey on hands,
I'm stuck in this moment, it never expands.

Ascending Shadows

Shadows stretch out like they're having a blast,
They reach for the sky, they run and they dance.
But when I step close, they cling to my shoe,
As if they are saying, 'We're not done with you!'

I jump to break free, but they hold me down tight,
These shadows are stubborn, they just want to fight.
With a flick of my wrist, I try to take flight,
But the shadows just giggle, 'You're grounded tonight!'

Tethered to the Ground

With a hop and a skip, I dream of the skies,
But my feet, like anchors, are fooling my flies.
I try to fly high, but I sink like a stone,
Just a grounded young thing in a world of my own.

My aspirations float, like balloons in a breeze,
But reality pulls them, it's all just a tease.
So here I remain, in this comical race,
Trying to soar with a grin on my face.

The Burden of Being

Being is tricky, like a wriggly worm,
It wiggles and giggles, then throws me a curve.
One minute I'm flying, the next I'm a rock,
The burden of living must come with a clock.

I carry my worries like bags on my back,
And trip on my laughter, oh what a whack!
But with every misstep, I just can't help but grin,
For the fun of this burden feels like a win!

When Laughter Turns Leaden

In jest we float, in giggles we leap,
But soon we trip, our joy's too deep.
With every chuckle, the weight just grows,
As humor's charm begins to doze.

We bounce about, like kittens in play,
Yet suddenly we sink, not okay!
The punchlines hit like heavy rocks,
Our laughter's lost in time's ticking clocks.

With every joke, a slackening limb,
As smiles fade fast, our hopes grow dim.
We wobble and wobble, but don't take flight,
What once was humor now gives a fright.

So here's to the giggles that could have soared,
Yet lingered too long, and now feel bored.
We aim for the sky but find the floor,
In laughter's chains, we can't take more.

The Strain of Stillness

We sit and chat, the clock strikes slow,
In silence we wait, though laughter's a-go.
But stillness weighs like a heavy stone,
Our voices echo, feeling alone.

The jokes we tell just float like lead,
No spark ignites, we hang by a thread.
With every pause the fun's on pause,
In quietude, the punchline jaws.

We stretch our smiles, but they feel tight,
Our bodies crumple, try as we might.
In fidgety motions, we seek the breeze,
Yet all we find are creaks and wheezes.

Here's to the waiting, the cringe of the chill,
As we face the tug of the stillness thrill.
With laughter's weight bearing down on our chest,
We cry for escape, but we're put to the test.

Submerged in Yearning

We dive into dreams, where jokes can flow,
Yet surface with sighs, feeling the low.
Our wishes float like boats in the night,
But laughter drowns, losing its light.

We reach for the punchlines lost in the tide,
But waves of woes, we cannot deride.
We giggle and gasp, but still seem to sink,
In depths of the mundane, we barely blink.

Our hopes bob along, like driftwood afloat,
But humor's a ship, lost without a coat.
We swim for the shore, but just can't get near,
With each grasp for joy, we taste only fear.

So here we are, in a sea of bad puns,
Where laughter's a race that never quite runs.
We want to emerge, but we're caught in the swirl,
As yearnings tug hard, in a watery whirl.

Beneath the Load of Time

Tick-tock the clock, the seconds drag,
With every chime, we lift a sag.
Humor's a weight strapped tight to our backs,
As laughter's lull begs for laughs on the racks.

We wander in circles, each smile feels forced,
With giggles but echoes, we're all out-sourced.
The jokes we concoct, like old circus tricks,
We've juggled our hearts, but lost all the kicks.

As time sags low, and wit starts to rust,
We ponder the punchlines left in the dust.
With every tick, the fun's slipping fast,
The laughter we cherished feels covered in cast.

So let's lift the weight, and tickle the strings,
Throw off the burden that boredom brings.
For beneath every hour, in silence we'll soar,
In the comical dance, we'll find evermore.

Tethered to the Floor

I tried to dance upon the stars,
But found I'm bound to this planet's bars.
My feet they sink into the ground,
I leap for joy, yet stay quite round.

A trampoline seemed like a plan,
But it just flung me back, oh man!
With every jump, I'd crash and cling,
To laws that keep me from the spring.

Chasing Clouds

I chased a cloud, it looked so light,
But slipped away, oh what a sight!
I leapt with hope to touch the sky,
Yet met a tree, and said goodbye.

The breeze it laughed, I tripped and fell,
Stumbling down, I could just yell!
I thought I soared, a bird in flight,
Instead, I'm grounded, oh what a plight!

Embracing Soil

I hoped to float like autumn leaves,
Instead, I'm stuck where dirt deceives.
The worms tell me it's comfy here,
So I'll just lounge without a fear.

With every step, I feel the pull,
The ground's so soft, it's quite the lull.
I argue with the rising moon,
Yet every night, I'm back by noon.

The Downward Spiral

Round and round, the world goes 'round,
 I try to rise, yet lose my ground.
Each twist and turn, my bladder leaks,
 The earth it laughs as I just squeak.

A rollercoaster, such great fun,
 Except I'm stuck at the bottom run.
Like a yo-yo in a clever game,
I bounce right back, but it's just a shame!

Loosening the Chains of Weight

I thought that lightness was the way,
But every snack just led to sway.
I'd give a giggle to float away,
Yet snack on chips, the price I pay.

I dream of flying, fanciful sights,
But gravity holds me through the nights.
To lose these chains, oh what a feat,
For now, I'll dance on wobbly feet.

Moments of Defiance Against the Weight

When you jump, do you hear?
The giggles of forces near.
Your toes tap against the sky,
As clouds wave and whisper, 'Fly!'

With each leap, the world feels light,
A daring dance, oh what a sight!
The ground grumbles in surprise,
While we twirl and spin, oh how time flies!

Gravity rolls her eyes in jest,
As we play and flirt with the best.
She tugs but we wriggle away,
Defying her pull in a daring ballet!

In sneakers and sandals we'd glide,
Through air, we will pirouette and slide.
Laughing at forces that would confine,
In defiance, we toast with a fizzy wine!

Resisting the Downward Drift

Oh, the floor feels like a plot,
A sticky trap, a sly hotshot.
I bounce on couches, defy the couch,
As cushions erupt, we laugh and slouch.

Chandeliers dance like they're on a spree,
While I twirl and giggle with glee.
The world may pull with all its might,
But I'm the star of this comical flight.

Tables quake as I hop around,
Each leap echoed in boisterous sound.
Let's waltz with a banana in hand,
A slippery slip, the best comic band!

Defying the urge to plummet or pout,
With every bounce, I've let it out.
The ground can wait, I'm too busy to drift,
For laughter is the ultimate gift!

Weightless Whispers

In a dreamlike state I float,
With jelly legs, I wiggle and tote.
A feather's dance, a sly ballet,
Swaying soft like kids at play.

'Come here!' the floor grumbles low,
But I'm flipping like a prospector's show.
Caught between a giggle and a sigh,
My heart races as I suddenly fly!

Gravity cackles, tries to draw near,
But I'm busy spinning without a fear.
Head over heels, I chuckle and sway,
Creating chuckles in my amusing ballet.

My mind's on a trampoline, skip and bound,
Where jokes float up, and smiles abound.
Defying the dip, I rise and slide,
In this playful world where we bide our pride!

The Pull of Solitude

In my chair I sit so snug,
Reading tales with a cozy hug.
But the couch whispers, 'Come on, roam!'
While my slippers sigh, 'Let's go back home.'

The walls stare, they don't look pleased,
As I wriggle and jiggle, slightly cheesed.
It's a riddle, a game, a fight for fun,
Me against the chair; who'll be the one?

The snacks laugh as I make my move,
With every nibble, I find my groove.
"Oh chair, you think you're so strong?"
But I bounce and bounce; it's where I belong!

Yet in this tug of war I cheer,
With humor and snacks, I have no fear.
For solitude holds a comical sway,
As laughter and snacks keep the blues at bay!

Anchored to the Sky

I tried to float, just be free,
But my shoes said, "Not for thee!"
I jumped up high, with all my might,
And landed hard, what a sight!

The trampoline just laughed at me,
As I soared far too clumsily.
With every bounce, I'd twist and shout,
But my feet said, "No way out!"

They say the clouds are fluffy, light,
But I felt heavy, what a fright!
I spread my arms, I tried to glide,
But down I came, an awkward slide!

The birds they laughed, they flew with ease,
I waved to them, cursing the breeze.
They circled back, just to say,
"Why don't you join us, just for play?"

Sinking in Stardust

I wished to dance on moonlit beams,
But tripped on shadows, not my dreams.
I wore a space suit, thought it sly,
Yet fell like lead, oh me, oh my!

A comet zoomed, said, "What a site!"
I waved back, but lost my flight.
With each mistake, I'd holler loud,
The universe just shook its cloud.

They told me, "Space is warm and bright,"
But I discovered, it's quite a fright.
With every step, I'd make a scene,
Stardust stuck to my jeans, how mean!

I tried to float, but sank instead,
My hopes like meteors – they fled.
So here I lie, a cosmic mess,
Laughing softly in this distress.

The Burden of the Ground

I dreamed of soaring, high and grand,
But here I sit, just on the land.
I packed my bags with hopes so bright,
Then tripped on roots, what a sight!

The weight of soil just clung to me,
While ants in lines danced joyfully.
I shouted loud, "Let's fly today!"
But earth replied, "Not your way!"

You see, my friends, I try my best,
To lift my feet and pass this test.
But every step feels like a load,
Like walking up a mountain road.

I'd love to skip through fields of glee,
Instead, I waddle, clumsily.
I laugh and sigh, enjoy the round,
For being stuck feels quite profound.

Heaviness in Freefall

I took a leap, thought I could fly,
But down I plummeted, oh my!
I flailed my arms, screamed to go up,
Yet smashed the ground, my poor luck!

A bird flew past, a feathered pro,
I shouted, "Teach me how to glow!"
It chirped back, "Take it easy there!"
But I just tangled in mid-air!

Each drop felt like my shoes had lead,
As giggles bubbled up instead.
I tumbled down from sky to earth,
In laughter found my own rebirth.

The clouds just waved, they knew my plight,
As I spun 'round, a funny sight.
With every crash, I'd laugh and say,
"Next time I'll just float away!"

Descending into Clarity

I tried to float, but oh, what a blunder,
Down like a rock, I plummeted under.
My thoughts were light, but my body was dense,
Why does sanity come at such expense?

A balloon in my hand chased dreams in the air,
But it popped with a bang, oh what a scare!
Like a bird I'll soar, I swear I will try,
But my feet are glued, my hopes stuck awry.

Bright minds might fly while I'm glued to the ground,
Every step feels like I'm lifting a mound.
Yet laughter erupts like a joyous parade,
As I tumble and stumble, my plans all remade.

So here I stand, not soaring or flapping,
But dancing on earth with my joy overlapping.
The world spins 'round—and I'm part of the jest,
I may not rise high, but at least I am best!

The Burden of Rising

I strapped on my wings, but they wobbled and creaked,
Thought I could fly, but my knees felt weak.
Up in the clouds, I had visions of glory,
Instead, I fell flat—oh, what a sad story!

A ladder of dreams took me high to the sky,
But it turned into taffy, and oh my, oh my!
I climbed and I climbed, but the steps turned to goo,
Now I tumble with giggles, my spirit askew.

The higher I reach, the more I get stuck,
It's a whimsical dance, or just bad luck?
But falling is funny, as it turns out,
In this slapstick ballet, there's joy all about!

So let's raise a toast to the skyward ambition,
With laughter and cheer, it's quite the tradition!
Though I may not float, I'll still wave my flag,
Life's lighter when you let go of the drag!

Shadows of a Dream

In a world of my dreams, I wanted to soar,
But my feet stayed planted—what a chore!
I chased after rainbows with mischief afoot,
But the ground pulled me back, and I laughed till I toot.

With clouds for my pillows, I'd nap in the sun,
While the world spins 'round like a long marathon run.
I tried to be light, but I still held my weight,
Oh, how this dream feels like a comical fate!

I twirled with the stars, but my head stayed down,
A jester on Earth in a whimsical gown.
The shadows were dancing, they giggled with glee,
In this circus of flops, I felt ever so free!

So here I will linger, a dreamer down low,
Transforming my stumbles to laughter and show.
With every misstep, I will always embrace,
The humor in falling, an unending grace!

Surrendering to the Forces

Once I aimed high, but flew like a lead,
My ambitions went plop, like a loaf of bread.
I jumped with a smile, seeking dizzy delight,
But all I got was a very flat flight!

I considered a parachute, but it went bare,
I fell with a thud—it was one joyous scare!
A suitcase of hope, it tipped over the brim,
Now it's packed with laughter, chances are slim.

Defying the odds, I giddily roll,
With gravity's laughter, I'm having a ball!
Why rise with a frown when the tumble is fun?
Let's dance with the forces—it's just begun!

So here's to the ground, where faces meet dirt,
In my comedy caper, I twirl and I flirt.
Embracing the splat, oh the fun that it brings,
Let's all be a part of these laughable things!

www.ingramcontent.com/pod-product-compliance
Lightning Source LLC
Chambersburg PA
CBHW051629160426
43209CB00004B/577